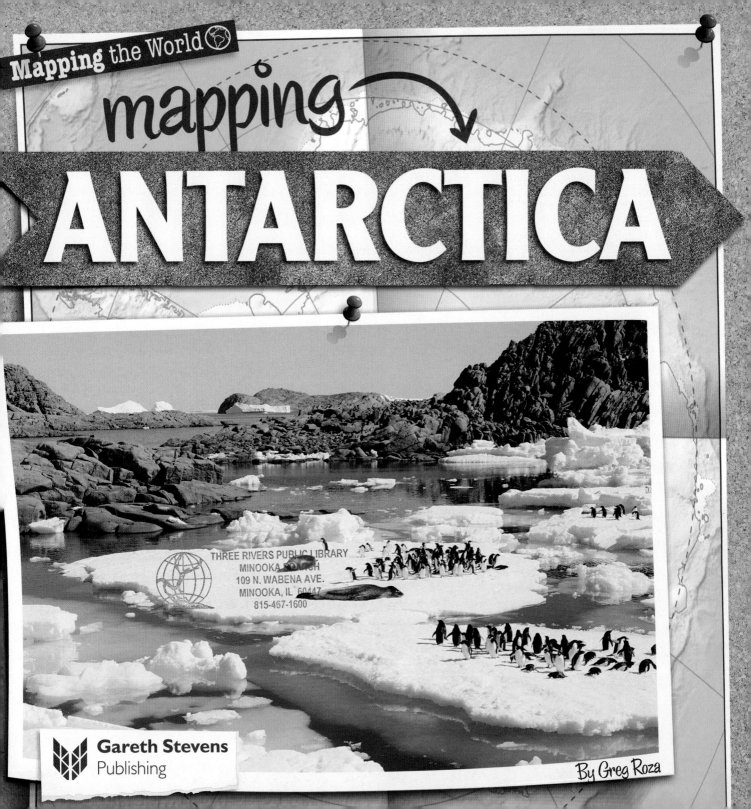

mapping
ANTARCTICA

Gareth Stevens
Publishing

By Greg Roza

Please visit our website, www.garethstevens.com. For a free color catalog of all our high-quality books, call toll free 1-800-542-2595 or fax 1-877-542-2596.

Library of Congress Cataloging-in-Publication Data

Roza, Greg.
 Mapping Antarctica / Greg Roza.
     pages cm. — (Mapping the world)
 Includes index.
 ISBN 978-1-4339-9095-3 (pbk.)
 ISBN 978-1-4339-9096-0 (6-pack)
 ISBN 978-1-4339-9094-6 (library binding)
 1. Maps—Antarctica—Juvenile literature. 2. Cartography—Antarctica—Juvenile literature. I. Title.
 GA357.R69 2014
 526.09989—dc23

                            2012049131

First Edition

Published in 2014 by
Gareth Stevens Publishing
111 East 14th Street, Suite 349
New York, NY 10003

Designer: Katelyn E. Reynolds
Editor: Kristen Rajczak

Photo credits: Cover, p. 1 (photo) Stockbyte/Thinkstock.com; cover, pp. 1, 21 (map) Alexrk2/Wikipedia.com; cover, pp. 1–24 (banner) kanate/Shutterstock.com; cover, pp. 1–24 (series elements and cork background) iStockphoto/Thinkstock.com; p. 5 Nations Online Project; p. 7 Lokal_Profil/Wikipedia.com; p. 9 (inset) Todd Sowers/NOAA/Wikipedia.com; p. 9 (main) NASA/Wikipedia.com; p. 11 (inset) Christopher Shuman, ICESat Deputy Project Scientist, Goddard Space Flight Center; p. 11 (main) Gordon Wiltsie/National Geographic/Getty Images; p. 13 (inset) Unites States Geological Survey; p. 13 (main) Doug Allan/Oxford Scientific/Getty Images; p. 15 (inset) Dimitri Torterat (Diti)/Wikipedia.com; p. 15 (main) Sue Flood/The Image Bank/Getty Images; p. 17 Zoonar/Thinkstock.com; p. 19 (inset) USGS/Science Source/Photo Researchers/Getty Images; p. 19 (main) Gaelen Marsden/Wikipedia.com.

Printed in the United States of America

CPSIA compliance information: Batch #CS13GS: For further information contact Gareth Stevens, New York, New York at 1-800-542-2595.

CONTENTS

Words in the glossary appear in **bold** type the first time they are used in the text.

THE COLD CONTINENT

Land was long thought to be at the southern end of the globe, but Antarctica wasn't truly discovered until around 1820. Today we know it's Earth's southernmost continent. The South Pole is located near the center of this frozen land.

Antarctica lies almost entirely within the Antarctic Circle, or **latitude** 66° 34′ South. Any area south of this latitude experiences at least 24 hours of sunlight once a year and 24 hours of darkness once a year. Some areas experience months with sun all the time and months with no sun at all.

Where in the World?

Long ago, Antarctica was a much warmer place. The landmass drifted to its current location over millions of years.

ANTARCTIC REGION

0   500   1000 Kilometers

0   500   1000 Miles

5

ANTARCTIC TERRITORIES

The territories of Antarctic land claimed by nations around the world resemble slices of pizza. That's because most borders on Antarctica follow straight lines of **longitude**. Seven countries have claimed sections of Antarctica. The claims of England, Chile, and Argentina overlap each other, though no disputes over land claims have arisen.

The United States and Russia haven't claimed land. However, because they helped explore the continent, they reserve the right to claim land in the future.

Where in the World?

In 1959, 12 nations signed the Antarctic Treaty. This treaty states that the Antarctic Continent will always be used for peaceful and scientific purposes. Since then, many other countries have agreed to the treaty.

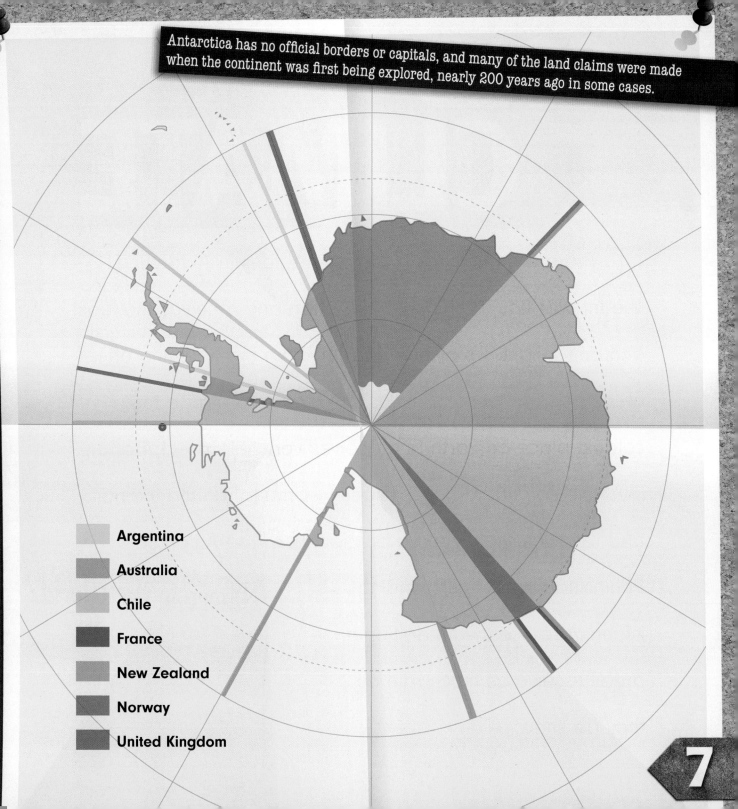

Argentina

Australia

Chile

France

New Zealand

Norway

United Kingdom

COLD CLIMATE

There are three main **climate** regions in Antarctica.

The interior has the highest **elevation** and receives the least annual sunlight. It's also separated from the warming effect of the ocean. Because of this, the interior region is the coldest place on Earth but receives very little **precipitation**.

The coastal region is slightly warmer than the interior and receives slightly more precipitation. The Antarctic Peninsula and the surrounding islands are even warmer. Some areas receive as much rain as they do snow.

Where in the World?

The coldest temperature ever recorded on Earth, −128.6°F (−89.2°C), occurred at Russia's Vostok Antarctic Research Station in 1983.

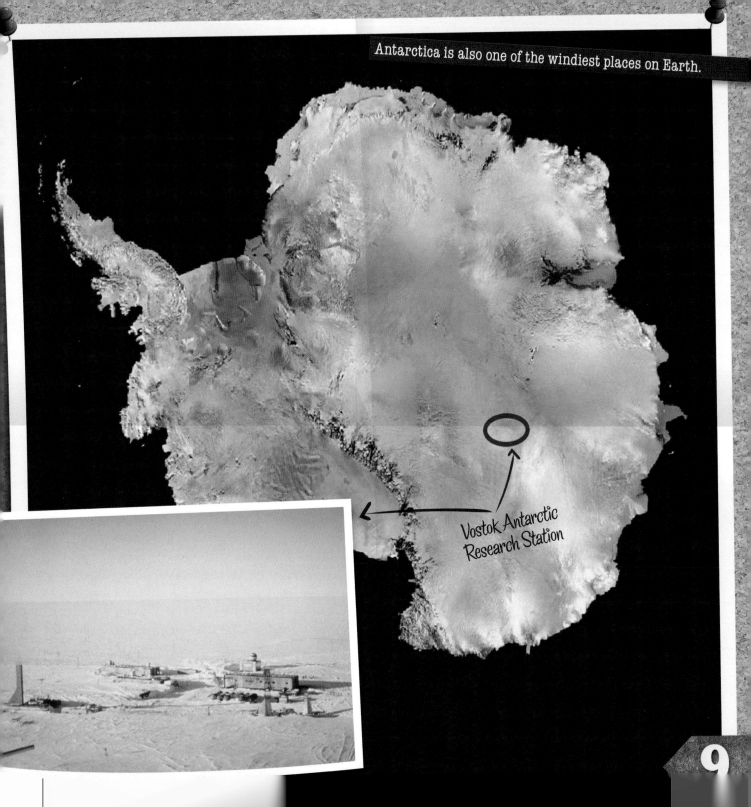

Antarctica is also one of the windiest places on Earth.

Vostok Antarctic
Research Station

SOUTHERNMOST MOUNTAINS

The Transantarctic Mountains are a long range that forms the border between East Antarctica and West Antarctica. The Ellsworth Mountains are the tallest range on Antarctica. At about 16,050 feet (4,890 m) tall, Vinson Massif is the tallest mountain of that range.

In 1958, Russian scientists discovered a giant mountain range in East Antarctica. However, they almost walked right over it without noticing. The Gamburtsev Mountains are buried beneath nearly 3 miles (4.8 km) of ice!

Where in the World?

The highest peaks of the Gamburtsev Mountain Range are about 15,000 feet (4,600 m) tall.

The colors of this map show the elevation differences across Antarctica in meters. The areas in red are the highest elevations, and the blues are the areas closest to sea level. The height of Vinson Massif, pictured below, would place it in a greenish-blue area on this map.

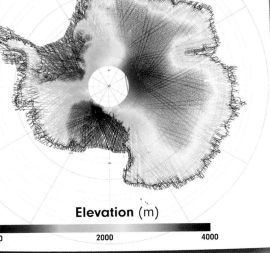

Elevation (m)

0   2000   4000

ANTARCTIC VOLCANOES

The Transantarctic Mountains include several inactive **volcanoes**. The South Sandwich Islands were created by underwater volcanoes. Volcanoes near the South Sandwich Islands are busy building new islands, but they're still underwater.

Ross Island was created by four volcanoes: Mount Erebus, Mount Terror, Mount Bird, and Hut Point Peninsula. Mount Erebus is the southernmost active volcano on the planet. It's one of just five volcanoes on Earth that feature a long-lasting lava lake in their crater.

Where in the World?

Near the tip of the Antarctic Peninsula is the horseshoe-shaped Deception Island. This island is actually a flooded, active volcano.

On the topographical map of Ross Island below, you can see how high Mount Erebus is! This still-active volcano may produce smoke and other hot matter.

Mount Erebus

ROSS ISLAND

GLACIERS AND ICE SHELVES

Glaciers cover nearly all Antarctica and make up about 90 percent of the total glacier ice on Earth. Only 5 percent of the Antarctic coastline is bare rock.

The places where the glaciers extend out over water are called ice shelves. These are thick layers of ice that float. The Ross Ice Shelf is the largest ice shelf in the world. It's about the size of Spain! The thickest part is 2,300 feet (701 m) thick.

Where in the World?

In 2000, a massive iceberg bigger than Massachusetts calved, or broke away, from the Ross Ice Shelf. It's the largest iceberg on record.

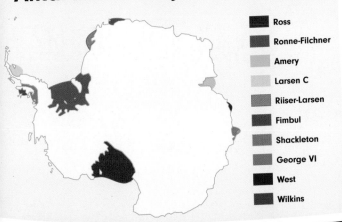

Antarctica's Major Ice Shelves

- Ross
- Ronne-Filchner
- Amery
- Larsen C
- Riiser-Larsen
- Fimbul
- Shackleton
- George VI
- West
- Wilkins

15

ANTARCTIC WILDLIFE

Despite being the coldest continent on Earth, Antarctica is home to some hardy animals. Most live on the coast and surrounding islands. Antarctica's most famous animal is the penguin. Other land animals include bugs, earthworms, and albatrosses. People have introduced other animals to the subantarctic region, the area just north of Antarctica. These include rats, mice, cats, sheep, and pigs.

The waters surrounding Antarctica support far more animals than live on the continent itself. These include whales, seals, fish, squid, and tiny shrimp-like animals called krill.

Where in the World?

In addition to animals, Antarctic wildlife includes plantlike water dwellers called algae, **lichens**, and two kinds of flowering plants.

Emperor penguins are the only animals that brave the winter on the open ice in Antarctica.

PEOPLE IN ANTARCTICA

Antarctica is one of the most interesting laboratories on Earth. Scientists from all over the world live and work in research stations throughout the continent. They study wildlife, **geology**, weather, **astronomy**, and the ocean, among other things.

McMurdo Station is a US research station that was built on Ross Island in 1955. It has about 85 buildings, including a firehouse and a power plant. It also has a landing strip built on an ice shelf. McMurdo Station is the largest community on Antarctica.

Where in the World?

American scientists have lived and worked at the Amundsen-Scott South Pole Station since 1956.

Ross
Ice
Shelf

McMurdo Station

Ross Island

Scott Coast

McMurdo Station is the closest thing Antarctica has to a city.

LAKE VOSTOK

Lake Vostok is no regular body of water. It's a lake the size of Lake Ontario that has been buried beneath more than 2 miles (3.2 km) of ice for at least 14 million years!

In the 1990s, Russian scientists began drilling into the ice above Lake Vostok. The deeper they drilled, the more they learned about Antarctica's—and Earth's—past. In 2012, the team reached the surface of the ancient body of water. In the near future, scientists will examine Lake Vostok to see if it contains unknown **microorganisms**.

Where in the World?

Lake Vostok is just one subglacial lake being studied. The British Antarctic Survey is trying to learn more about Lake Ellsworth, while mainly US scientists are studying Whillans Ice Stream.

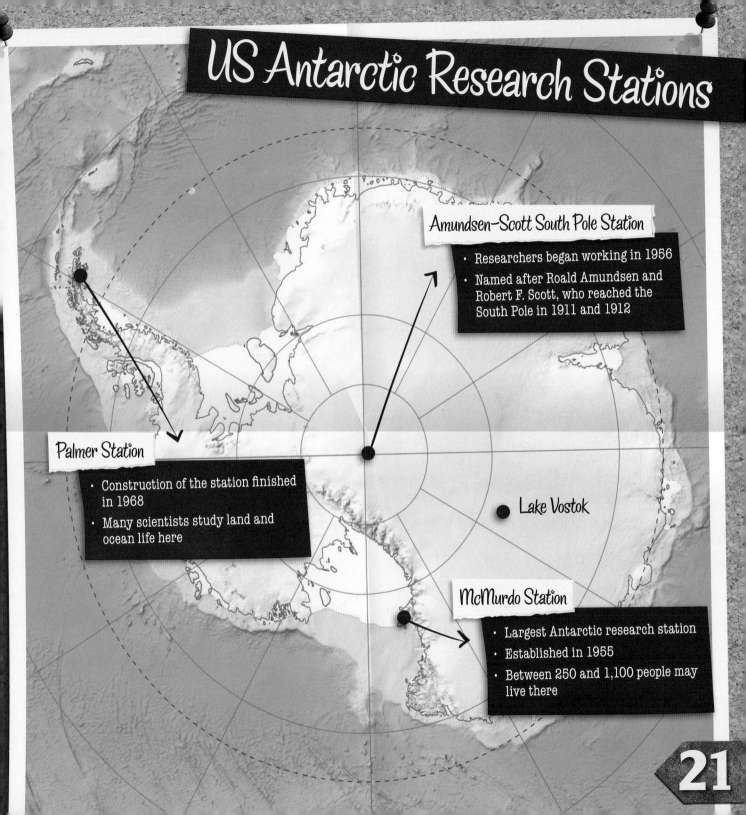

US Antarctic Research Stations

Amundsen–Scott South Pole Station

- Researchers began working in 1956
- Named after Roald Amundsen and Robert F. Scott, who reached the South Pole in 1911 and 1912

Palmer Station

- Construction of the station finished in 1968
- Many scientists study land and ocean life here

Lake Vostok

McMurdo Station

- Largest Antarctic research station
- Established in 1955
- Between 250 and 1,100 people may live there

GLOSSARY

astronomy: the study of the universe

climate: the average weather conditions of a place over a period of time

elevation: height above sea level

geology: the science that studies the history of Earth and its life as recorded in rocks

glacier: a large body of ice and snow pressed tightly together that moves slowly forward

latitude: an imaginary line that circles Earth and is always the same distance north or south of the equator

lichen: a life-form made up of a fungus and an alga growing together

longitude: an imaginary line that begins at one pole and ends at the other

microorganism: a living thing that can only be seen through a microscope

precipitation: rain, snow, hail, and sleet

volcano: an opening in a planet's surface through which hot, liquid rock sometimes flows

FOR MORE INFORMATION

Books

Latta, Sara L. *Ice Scientist: Careers in the Frozen Antarctic*. Berkeley Heights, NJ: Enslow Publishers, 2009.

Meinking, Mary. *Who Counts the Penguins? Working in Antarctica*. Chicago, IL: Raintree, 2011.

Schaefer, A. R. *Spotlight on Antarctica*. Mankato, MN: Capstone Press, 2011.

Websites

Antarctica
www.nhm.ac.uk/nature-online/earth/antarctica/index.html
Read more information about Earth's coldest continent and see more maps of it.

Discover Antarctica
ngm.nationalgeographic.com/ngm/antarctica/
Use an interactive map to see videos, read articles, and learn about Antarctic animals.

INDEX